NINA'S MAGIC

NINA'S MAGIC

written and illustrated by
Lisa Kirsten Butenhoff

LANDMARK EDITIONS, INC.

P.O. Box 4469 • 1402 Kansas Avenue • Kansas City, Missouri 64127
(816) 241-4919

Dedicated to:
Mom, Dad,
and my brother David
for their love and support.

Second Printing

COPYRIGHT © 1992 BY LISA KIRSTEN BUTENHOFF

International Standard Book Number: 0-933849-40-0 (LIB.BDG.)

Library of Congress Cataloging-in-Publication Data
Butenhoff, Lisa Kirsten, 1977-
  Nina's magic / written and illustrated by Lisa Kirsten Butenhoff.
  p.   cm.
  Summary: When Nina discovers that the things she paints with her new watercolors
become real, she uses her magic to save the people of her small Russian village from
hunger and oppression.
  ISBN 0-933849-40-0 (lib.bdg. : acid free)
  1. Children's writings,   2. Children's art—United
  American.   States.
  [1. Painting—Fiction.   2. Artists—Fiction.
  3. Magic—Fiction.   4. Soviet Union—Fiction.
  5. Children's writings.   6. Children's art.]
  I. Title.
PZ7.B9694Ni   1992
[Fic]—dc20
                                              92-18293
                                              CIP
                                              AC

Editorial Coordinator: Nancy R. Thatch
Creative Coordinator: David Melton

Printed in the United States of America

Landmark Editions, Inc.
P.O. Box 4469
1402 Kansas Avenue
Kansas City, Missouri 64127
(816) 241-4919

NINA'S MAGIC

When Lisa Butenhoff traveled to Russia with her family, she was impressed by the friendliness of the people she met. She found the Russians to be very caring and generous with each other and with visitors who came into their homes.

After Lisa returned to the United States, she wanted to find a way of expressing her thanks to her Russian friends for the many kindnesses they had extended to her and her family. The result is NINA'S MAGIC, a book that captures the style and appearance of an Old-World folk tale.

Within the story, the generosity of the Russian people is personified by a young girl whose special gifts help improve the lives of the people of her village. There is also a soft, lyrical quality in Lisa's writing and beautiful water-color illustrations that reflects her own gentle, thoughtful nature.

In NINA'S MAGIC, Lisa has created a loving and meaningful "thank you" — one of touching sensitivity and appreciation.

Read, look, and enjoy.

— David Melton
Creative Coordinator
Landmark Editions, Inc.

NINA'S MAGIC

Many years ago in the faraway lands of northern Russia, there was a village called Holodnie. The small hamlet lay in the path of the great North Wind where winters are long and bitter with cold.

Each year the villagers worked hard to prepare for the harsh winter they knew would come. They mended the roofs of their worn little houses and patched the cracks in the walls. They chopped down trees and split timber into firewood. And they harvested the golden wheat and grew plenty of vegetables to store for the cold months ahead.

Then hard times came to Holodnie. One day soldiers marched into the village. They rounded up all the strong young men and took them away to work camps. Overnight, Holodnie became a village of old men, women and children, left on their own to do the work and survive as best they could.

To make matters worse, the rains did not fall for several summers, and a terrible drought covered the land. Wheat withered in the fields and vegetables would not grow in the gardens. The villagers' stomachs ached with hunger, for there were few potatoes left and not enough wheat to make bread.

Then a magical thing happened in Holodnie — something so mysterious that to this day, the villagers still talk about it in wonder and amazement.

It all began in an old wooden house that stood at the very edge of the village. Frozen by fierce winds and deep snow, the small dwelling clung to the earth amid the dark forest that surrounded it. Here, a young girl named Nina lived with her old grandmother.

One cold night the wind cried louder than ever and beat against the house. Nina and her grandmother sat near the *pechka and tried to keep warm. As her grandmother knitted a shawl, the girl huddled even closer to the hearth and listened to the sounds of the wind.

"Grandmother," Nina asked, "why does the wind moan so loudly?"

The old woman looked up from her knitting and replied, "Old North Wind moans because it is cold. It wants to come inside where it is warm."

"It's not very warm in here tonight," Nina said with a shiver.

"That is because Old North Wind has found all the cracks in the walls and is sneaking inside without being invited."

"If my papa were here, he would fix the walls," Nina said.

"Yes, he would," her grandmother agreed. "Your papa is a fine carpenter. He is also stronger than I am and able to chop big logs for the pechka. If he were here, there would be plenty of firewood, and our house would stay warm."

"Papa is a good artist, too," Nina said. "The pictures he painted looked so real, I felt I could step into them. I wish I had a set of paints like Papa's. If I did, Grandmother, I would paint a picture for you right now. I could, you know. Papa showed me how to mix colors and paint with them."

"It pleases me that you remember your papa so well," her grandmother smiled.

"I also remember the day the soldiers came and took Papa and the other men away," Nina recalled sadly.

"That was a bad day," her grandmother said quietly.

"And I remember when Mama left us to go search for him," Nina sighed.

"That was a long time ago, child. Almost three years have passed."

The howl of the wind made Nina feel even sadder. She shivered again and tears filled her eyes. She longed to see her parents and wished her family could be together again.

"Grandmother," she said softly, "will Mama ever find Papa?"

The old woman reached down and stroked Nina's hair. "We can only hope she will," she answered. Then she changed the subject to try to cheer the girl.

"Here, Nina," she said as she placed the shawl snugly around her granddaughter's shoulders. "I have just finished this for you. It will keep you warm and safe from the cold. Old North Wind will not be able to get through your nice new shawl."

*pech•ka (pech′ kə), a large stove-oven used for cooking, baking, and the heating of the house. The flat roof of the stove also serves as a bed.

"Oh, thank you, Grandmother! It's beautiful!" Nina exclaimed, feeling the warmth wrapped around her.

"And now, child," the old woman said, "it is time for bed."

Nina undressed and slipped into her nightgown. Then she climbed up onto the warm roof of the pechka where she and her grandmother slept every night.

"Grandmother," Nina asked, "do you think Mama and Papa miss us as much as we miss them?"

"I know they miss us every day and think of us every night," her grandmother assured her.

"Tonight I will try to think warm thoughts for Mama and Papa," Nina said, "because I am afraid they may be cold like us."

"That is a good idea," her grandmother said. "I will think warm thoughts with you." Then the old woman blew out the flame in the lamp, climbed up into bed beside Nina, and soon fell asleep.

Nina lay awake for a long time thinking about her parents. She tried to imagine them safe and warm on such a cold night as this. The young girl could not understand why people in the government would want to take her father so far away from his family. Finally, Nina became drowsy and drifted into sleep.

All night long the fierce wind blew drifts of snow against the tired house. But by morning the wind had stopped and the skies were clear.

Nina was awakened by the sound of wood being chopped. She looked out the window. Her grandmother was wielding the axe with all the strength the old woman could muster. The girl dressed quickly and hurried outside.

"Good morning, Nina," her grandmother called out. "Come, help me load this wood onto the sled. On our way to the village, we will stop by Maria's house and leave firewood for her."

"Is Maria out of wood?" Nina asked.

"She has not been well," her grandmother replied. "I'm sure she will need more wood."

After a breakfast of hot *kasha, Nina and her grandmother set out, pulling the rickety old sled behind them. The air was so cold, Nina thought her breath might freeze and fall to the ground in icicles.

When they came to Maria's house, the girl helped her grandmother unload the wood and stack it neatly beside the door.

"Do not mention to Maria that we brought wood for her," the grandmother cautioned.

"But, won't she know who left it?" Nina asked.

"Yes," her grandmother replied, "but we never give gifts to people because we expect them to thank us. We give to others for the pleasure of giving."

*ka•sha (ka′ shə), a cereal made of coarse grains of buckwheat or barley that are crushed and cooked.

11

The old woman reached out her hand and knocked.

Maria opened the door and welcomed them. "Nina! Olga! Come in out of the cold," she said. "I will make some tea. It will warm you both."

"That would be kind of you," the grandmother said as she and Nina stepped inside. "But do not bother, for we cannot stay long enough to drink the tea. We must get to the store before all the food is gone."

"Each day it gets worse," Maria said, shaking her head. "Food must be scarce everywhere in Russia. By the time the supply train reaches Holodnie, there is never enough left for us."

"Are you feeling better today?" the grandmother asked.

"Not much," Maria admitted. "I miss my husband, too, and little Sasha wonders where his papa is."

Nina looked over at the small boy who stood by the stove.

"Nina misses her parents also," the grandmother said. Then she leaned forward and asked Maria, "Have you heard any news?"

Maria's answer was spoken in whispers, kept so low that Nina could not make out the words. It was always like that when adults talked about missing people or the government.

So Nina left the two women to their conversation and looked at Sasha. The boy's clothing was worn and patched. Only a pair of frayed stockings protected his feet from the cold. Nina couldn't help but notice how thin the boy was and how he shivered. She wished she had a cup of warm milk to give to the child right now.

Nina smiled at Sasha, and he smiled back shyly. But when she said, "Hi, Sasha," and started toward him, the boy giggled and darted behind a chair.

Nina tip-toed quietly across the room and began a hide-and-seek game. "Where is Sasha?" she said. "Where is Sasha?" When she suddenly peeked over the back of the chair and touched the boy on top of his head, he laughed and jumped up. Then he ran across the room and wrapped his arms around his mother's legs.

"Sasha is such a shy child," explained Maria.

"He will not be so shy when he gets to know us better," the grandmother said, and she smiled at Sasha and patted his shoulder. Then she walked toward the door and motioned for Nina to follow. "Come," she said, "we must go."

Nina gave Maria a hug and waved to Sasha. Then she stepped outside and closed the door behind her.

The old woman and the girl made their way toward the village. Before long they arrived at the store where a crowd of villagers had already gathered.

"Hurry, Nina," the grandmother said, "let's get inside and take our place in the line."

Suddenly a young girl rushed up to them. "Hi, Nina!" she said. It was Katya, Nina's best friend.

"Katya!" laughed Nina.

"I hoped I would see you before I left the village," Katya told her.

"Why are you leaving?" Nina asked in concern.

"Times are so bad here," explained Katya. "My mother is sending me to live with my aunt and uncle until things get better. We have so little food, and the train brought even fewer supplies this time."

"Did it bring enough flour and potatoes?" Nina's grandmother asked anxiously.

"I don't know, but all the meat is gone," replied Katya.

The old woman sighed and shook her head in disappointment, then turned to talk with the other women.

"The train did bring something very pretty," Katya whispered excitedly to Nina.

"What?" Nina wanted to know.

"A large roll of bright green cloth!" replied Katya. "I hoped Mama could buy some to make a new dress for me. But she said, 'No, the material is too expensive.' "

Nina turned and saw a woman hold up a piece of the cloth.

"Oh!" exclaimed Nina. "It *is* beautiful!"

"If I were rich," Katya said dreamily, "I would buy the whole roll and give half of it to you."

Nina smiled as she imagined herself in a dress made from the cloth. Then she thought about a coat of green, too — one she could wear with her pretty new shawl.

Nina had been eager to show everyone her shawl. But now, standing next to Katya, she suddenly felt ashamed of having something that nice. Katya had nothing so fine. Her friend wore a faded coat that was too small for her and a dress that had been patched many times.

After a while the grandmother called Nina to help carry supplies to the sled.

"At least I got a sack of potatoes and some flour, and even a bit of tea and sugar," the old woman said.

After the sled was loaded, Nina turned and gave Katya a hug. "I will miss you," she said to her friend.

"I will miss you, too," Katya said, and she waved good-bye sadly.

As Nina and her grandmother trudged toward home, the gray sky above them darkened. Flurries of snow began to fill the air, and the wind blew colder.

"We must hurry," the old woman said. "A bad storm is coming."

By the time they reached home, Nina and her grandmother were so cold, they could hardly move. As soon as the supplies were carried inside, the grandmother placed more wood in the pechka. Then she prepared the *samovar for tea and began to cut up potatoes to make soup.

Outside, the wind moaned even louder than it had the night before. Suddenly, Nina thought she heard something else — a knocking sound at the door.

"Grandmother, what was that noise?" she asked.

"It was only Old North Wind trying to get in."

"No," Nina insisted, "it's not the wind. I think someone is at our door."

The knocking sounded again.

"You're right!" exclaimed her grandmother. "But, who would be out on such a night as this?" she wondered as she hurried across the room.

When the grandmother opened the door, a blast of icy wind blew into the house and an old man stumbled inside. His fur hat and long overcoat were caked with snow. His beard was frozen with ice. It looked as if Grandfather Frost had stepped right out of a Russian fairy tale.

"Nina, come quickly!" the grandmother called. And the two of them helped the old man to a chair by the pechka.

"Forgive me for intruding," their visitor said weakly as he slumped into the chair. "I am a traveler caught in the storm. I need a few moments to rest in the warmth of your home."

"You are welcome here," the grandmother told him.

"And you are very kind," he said.

The grandmother gave the man a cup of hot tea. When the potato soup was ready, she placed three steaming bowlfuls on the table. Then she sat down with Nina and their visitor to eat.

"I am sorry we cannot offer you more," the old woman said.

"To me, this hot soup is like a feast," the man replied and smiled kindly.

After supper the stranger told wonderful stories to Nina and her grandmother. He spoke of princes and princesses, of castles and dragons. Finally, he told them about faraway places where the winters are as warm as summer and flowers grow all year long.

"Have you seen such places?" Nina asked.

"I have been to many lands," he replied.

"What is the most wonderful place you have ever been?" Nina asked eagerly.

The old man looked directly at the girl and smiled. "The most wonderful place I have ever been is inside this house with you and your grandmother," he answered.

Nina did not understand what he meant. But before she could ask him, her grandmother said, "The hour is late. It is time for bed."

*sam•o•var (sam′ ə vär), a metal urn used for heating water for tea.

Nina helped her grandmother make a bed of blankets on the other side of the pechka for their visitor. The tired old man thanked them as he crawled between the warm covers.

Nina and her grandmother were tired too. Soon they were settled beside each other in their own bed.

"Grandmother," said Nina, "I wish I could make everyone in Holodnie warm and happy like the people in the old man's stories."

"Now I know I have come to the right house," the old man said softly.

That night the fire died down, but Nina did not feel the cold. She was warmed by amazing dreams of the sun-filled places the old man had told her about.

Early the next morning, Nina's grandmother got out of bed and added logs to the pechka. As the dry wood crackled into flames, she noticed their visitor's bed was empty.

The grandmother hurried to the window and looked outside. The blizzard still raged furiously, but their visitor was nowhere in sight. The old man was gone.

"How strange that he would leave without telling us good-bye," the old woman said to herself.

Then she heard Nina say, "Grandmother, where did this box come from?"

The grandmother turned and saw Nina was holding up a small wooden box. It was green with a gold and purple design on its lid.

"I have never seen that box before," the old woman replied. "Open it, and let's see what is inside."

Nina carefully unhooked the latch and raised the lid.

"Oh, Grandmother!" she exclaimed. "It's a box of water colors — just like the ones Papa had. And there's a brush too. But, how did they get here?"

"The old man must have left them for you," her grandmother replied.

"Did you tell him I wanted a set of paints?" Nina asked.

"No," her grandmother answered.

"Neither did I," Nina said in amazement. "I wonder how he knew?"

Nina quickly ate breakfast, for she could hardly wait to use the paints. Then she hurriedly filled a jar with water and placed it on the table beside a stack of paper.

"What shall I paint first, Grandmother?" Nina asked as she eagerly dipped the brush into the water.

"Whatever you like, child," the old woman replied.

Nina looked toward the window. All she could see outside was falling snow. In an instant she knew what she wanted to paint, and she began to mix the water with the colors.

Nina painted for some time. When she had finished, she showed the picture to her grandmother. It was a colorful scene of the village of Holodnie as it might appear on a bright, sunny day.

"This is very good," her grandmother smiled. Suddenly a ray of sunlight streamed through the window and caught the old woman's attention. "Look, Nina," she said, "it has stopped snowing, and the sun is shining here too."

Nina and her grandmother hurried to the window for a better look. It was a beautiful day outside! All the storm clouds had disappeared. The sunlight glistened and sparkled on the snow. And the houses of Holodnie were in clear view.

"Now the village looks just like your painting," the grandmother said.

"Yes, it does," Nina agreed. "Isn't that strange."

That night Nina had an unusual dream that was filled with warm, glowing colors. Yellows, oranges, and reds swirled around her and flowed through the air like the stripes of a rainbow. When Nina moved her hand to the right, a swash of red rushed before her eyes. When she moved her hand to the left, a band of orange streaked past her. And if she raised both hands, yellow mixed with the orange and red, and Nina could feel the warmth of a summer's day surround her.

When Nina awakened the warmth was gone. She shivered and snuggled farther under the blankets while her grandmother added wood to the pechka.

"Good morning, child," the old woman greeted her.

"Oh, Grandmother!" exclaimed Nina as she got out of bed and wrapped her shawl snugly around her shoulders. "I had the most wonderful dream last night. I was surrounded by beautiful colors, and when I mixed them together, I felt warm all over!"

"Ah," replied her grandmother, "I would like to have such a dream right now. I need something to warm my old bones on this cold morning."

"I can show you what my dream looked like," Nina offered eagerly.

While her grandmother watched, Nina took a sheet of paper and began to paint. Swirls of bright colors — reds, yellows, and oranges — flowed across the paper.

"Nina," the grandmother said, "the room is getting warmer."

"So it is," Nina agreed.

The old woman held her hand above the picture, and her eyes grew wide with wonder. "The heat is coming from your painting!" she exclaimed.

"But, how is that possible?" Nina asked in amazement.

"I do not know," her grandmother replied. "But it is happening. Yesterday you painted a sunny day and the blizzard stopped. This morning you painted a picture of bright colors, and our house became warmer.

"Nina," her grandmother smiled, "I think the old man left some truly amazing water colors for you! Whatever you paint with those colors becomes real."

"I think I will paint another picture and see what happens," Nina said.

Nina immediately thought of Maria and little Sasha in their cold house. She took another sheet of paper and painted a pechka that had a warm, glowing fire inside it. When the picture was finished, she and her grandmother hurried to the window and looked outside. They saw thick smoke rising from the chimney of Maria's house.

"Oh, Grandmother, you were right!" Nina exclaimed. "The things I paint do become real! It is like magic!"

The young girl and the old woman were so excited, they laughed and danced about the room.

Then Nina had another idea. This time she painted new coats, and mittens, and boots for Maria and Sasha. And her imagination did not stop there. She painted a cow so Sasha could have plenty of warm milk to drink.

Nina and her grandmother rushed to the window for another look. They saw Maria and Sasha had stepped outside, and they were dressed in their new clothing. The boy and his mother kept looking up and down the road, trying to see who had left the wonderful presents. And when they turned and saw the cow, Sasha laughed with delight; Maria was completely bewildered. Of course, all this pleased Nina and her grandmother even more.

Then Nina remembered Katya's faded coat and ragged dress. So she painted a new coat and dress for Katya, made of the beautiful green material her friend had admired. And she painted the cupboards in Katya's house with the shelves overflowing with food.

"Now Katya will not have to go live with her aunt and uncle," Nina said with a happy smile.

During the rest of the day, Nina painted one picture after another. Before she stopped, all the villagers were outfitted in warm clothes and sturdy boots. The shelves of every house were filled with potatoes and onions, and cabbages and beets, and flour to make bread. Even sugar, salt, and meat had suddenly appeared in the cupboards. And there was plenty of oil for cooking and kerosene for lamps.

All the leaky roofs, broken shutters and cracked walls of the houses in Holodnie were repaired. And every woodpile was stacked high with enough logs to last the whole winter.

Nina was overjoyed to see smoke billowing from all the chimneys. And her heart was touched by the warm glow of lamps that shone from the windows of the snug little houses. It had been a wonderful day for Nina. She had painted quickly and skillfully to give her friends the gifts they needed.

But toward evening Nina became very tired. And that's when the accident happened. Nina's elbow nudged the jar of water and knocked it over. The liquid poured all over one of the pictures.

"Oh, come look!" her grandmother called. "There is water flooding into the valley near the Propov house!"

Nina ran to the window to see for herself. Sure enough, where there once had been an open meadow, a wide blue lake had formed. Although the water sent the members of the Propov family scurrying up the hill, as it turned out, no harm was done to them or their house.

The result of the accident pleased Nina. She had always wanted a lake nearby where she could swim in the summer and ice skate in wintertime.

In her last picture of the day, Nina painted a warm coat and boots for her grandmother.

"Thank you, Nina," her grandmother said as she buttoned up her new coat. "It feels so soft and warm. Why don't you paint a pretty warm coat for yourself, too," the old woman suggested.

Nina became very quiet for a few moments. Then she said, "I don't think the old man intended for me to paint things I want. I believe he wanted me to use the paints to make things people really need. Besides, my coat still fits me, and it is not too badly worn."

That night Nina hoped she would have another dream of bright and beautiful colors, but it was not to be. This time she dreamed in shades of dull grays and browns. The cold colors chilled her and filled her with sadness. Then dark images began to appear in her dream.

Nina saw drab buildings that were surrounded by a tall, barb wire fence. A woman walked up to the fence and pleaded with guards to let her see one of the workers. Suddenly a man came out of one of the buildings. He waved to the woman and ran toward her. But before he could reach the fence, the guards stopped him and forced him back.

When Nina awakened, she found her eyes were filled with tears. She realized that the woman at the fence was her mother. The man the guards had stopped was her father. Her mother had found the work camp where her father and the other men were being held prisoners.

Nina wiped her eyes and crawled down from the pechka. She hurried to the table and lighted the lamp. Then she took a deep breath and began to create a picture. First, she painted the fence with its sharp barbs of wire. Then she added a high gate with guards standing at the entrance.

The girl shivered with excitement at what she was about to try. She dripped brushfuls of water onto the paper and watched as the images in the picture blurred and faded. When she swirled the water back and forth, the gate and the guards dissolved and disappeared. She painted the workers next as they came out of the buildings and walked through the opening in the fence.

Nina's excitement grew as she placed another sheet of paper before her. With each stroke of her brush, the girl painted the images she had in her mind. First, a train appeared in the picture. Then all the men from Holodnie were shown as they boarded the train, one by one. Nina eagerly dipped her brush into the paints once again, ready to add the two most important people to the picture — her mother and father.

It was then Nina became alarmed! She had been working so hard, she had not noticed that the paints were almost gone. In desperation she pressed the brush firmly down into the tray, trying to soak up the last bits of color. With those few drops, she painted the figures of her parents as they boarded the train.

Still Nina was concerned. All the other passengers in the painting were easy to see. But the images of her mother and father were pale and gray as if they were standing in a misty fog.

What if her parents weren't painted with enough color to make the magic work! Even worse, Nina still had to show the train stopping at the station in Holodnie. How could she do all that when there was no more paint?

As Nina frantically searched her mind for an idea, she noticed her grandmother's sewing basket on the corner of the table. She reached into it and quickly drew out a pair of scissors. Then she carefully cut out the train with its load of passengers and placed it on the very first painting she had done — the one of the sun-filled village of Holodnie.

Nina wondered if the magic would also work when one picture was placed over another. She hoped with all her heart that it would.

Early morning light now streamed through the window. Nina had painted most of the night, but she was too nervous to just sit and wait to find out if the magic had worked.

"Wake up, Grandmother!" she called. "We must dress quickly."

"Why?" her grandmother asked sleepily.

"We must go to the station to meet the train!" replied Nina.

"But the supply train will not come to Holodnie for another two weeks," the old woman said.

"This is a different kind of train!" Nina explained excitedly. "Hurry! We must be at the station when it arrives!"

The grandmother did not understand, but Nina was so insistent, the old woman got out of bed and dressed. Then she put on her new coat and boots and followed her granddaughter toward the village, trying her best to keep up.

"Hurry, Grandmother!" Nina kept calling as she raced ahead.

"There will be no train today," the grandmother repeated again and again. But she stopped talking when she heard the sound of a whistle and saw a pillar of black smoke billowing into the air.

"I told you, Grandmother!" Nina exclaimed. "You see, the train is almost to the village!"

That made the old woman quicken her steps. By the time she and Nina reached the station, the train had already pulled to a stop. All the villagers had gathered on the platform, eager to find out what was happening.

When the first passenger stepped down from the train, the villagers gasped in astonishment. It was Maria's husband. He saw his wife and hurried over to embrace her. Then he picked up little Sasha and held the boy tightly in his arms.

As each man got off the train, his family saw him and called out his name. There was much laughter and tears as the villagers hugged and kissed their returning loved ones. It was a joyous scene of homecoming and families reunited!

Nina ran back and forth, anxiously searching for her parents. She could not find them anywhere. After all the passengers were off the train and the families had left the station, Nina and her grandmother stood alone on the empty platform.

"But, where are your papa and mama?" the grandmother asked in disappointment.

"There wasn't enough paint to finish them," Nina explained sadly.

When the train started to move away, Nina leaned against her grandmother. The old woman slipped her arm around her granddaughter and tried to comfort the child.

"If there had been only a few more drops of paint, Mama and Papa would be here right now," said Nina, and tears swelled in her eyes and began to run down her cheeks.

Suddenly the train jolted to a stop. At the end of the platform, two passengers stepped off the last coach. Nina could not tell who they were. All she saw were two gray silhouettes standing in the misty steam that poured from the engine.

But something about the figures seemed familiar to Nina, and she started walking toward them. The closer she got to them, the clearer the images became. Suddenly she stopped and gasped with joy.

"Mama! Papa!" Nina cried out. And she ran the length of the platform and rushed into her parents' waiting arms.

Many years passed, but the people of Holodnie never forgot the unusual events that took place that cold winter long ago. The villagers always spoke in wonder about the gifts they received and the mysterious train that brought the men home to their families. But they could not explain how those marvelous things happened.

Only Nina and her grandmother ever knew the truth, and they chose to remain silent. They never told anyone about the old man who came in from the storm — an old man who left a special box of paints with a young girl because he knew she cared enough to share the magic of the colors with her friends.

Chandrasekhar
age 9

Anika Thomas
age 13

Cara Reichel
age 15

Jonathan Kahn
age 9

Adam Moore
age 9

Leslie A MacKeen
age 9

Elizabeth Haidle
age 13

Amy Hagstrom
age 9

Isaac Whitlatch
age 11

Dav Pilkey
age 19

by Aruna Chandrasekhar, age 9
Houston, Texas

A touching and timely story! When the lives of many otters are threatened by a huge oil spill, a group of concerned people come to their rescue. Wonderful illustrations.
Printed Full Color
ISBN 0-933849-33-8

by Anika D. Thomas, age 13
Pittsburgh, Pennsylvania

A compelling autobiography! A young girl's heartrending account of growing up in a tough, inner-city neighborhood. The illustrations match the mood of this gripping story.
Printed Two Colors
ISBN 0-933849-34-6

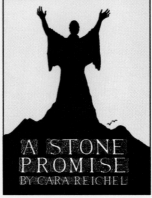

by Cara Reichel, age 15
Rome, Georgia

Elegant and eloquent! A young stonecutter vows to create a great statue for his impoverished village. But his fame almost stops him from fulfilling that promise.
Printed Two Colors
ISBN 0-933849-35-4

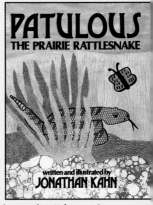

by Jonathan Kahn, age 9
Richmond Heights, Ohio

A fascinating nature story! While Patulous, a prairie rattlesnake, searches for food, he must try to avoid the claws and fangs of his own enemies.
Printed Full Color
ISBN 0-933849-36-2

by Adam Moore, age 9
Broken Arrow, Oklahoma

A remarkable true story! When Adam was eight years old, he fell and ran an arrow into his head. With rare insight and humor, he tells of his ordeal and his amazing recovery.
Printed Two Colors
ISBN 0-933849-24-9

by Michael Aushenker, age 19
Ithaca, New York

Chomp! Chomp! When Arthur forgets to feed his goat, the animal eats everything in sight. A very funny story — good to the last bite. The illustrations are terrific.
Printed Full Color
ISBN 0-933849-28-1

by Leslie Ann MacKeen, age 9
Winston-Salem, North Carolina

Loaded with fun and puns! When Jeremiah T. Fitz's car stops running, several animals offer suggestions for fixing it. The results are hilarious. The illustrations are charming.
Printed Full Color
ISBN 0-933849-19-2

by Elizabeth Haidle, age 13
Beaverton, Oregon

A very touching story! The grumpiest Elfkin learns to cherish the friendship of others after he helps an injured snail and befriends an orphaned boy. Absolutely beautiful.
Printed Full Color
ISBN 0-933849-20-6

by Amy Hagstrom, age 9
Portola, California

An exciting western! When a boy and an old Indian try to save a herd of wild ponies, they discover a lost canyon and see the mystical vision of the Great White Stallion.
Printed Full Color
ISBN 0-933849-15-X

by Isaac Whitlatch, age 11
Casper, Wyoming

The true confessions of a devout vegetable hater! Isaac tells ways to avoid and dispose of the "slimy green things." His colorful illustrations provide a salad of laughter and mirth.
Printed Full Color
ISBN 0-933849-16-8

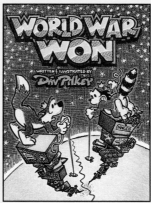

by Dav Pilkey, age 19
Cleveland, Ohio

A thought-provoking parable! Two kings halt an arms race and learn to live in peace. This outstanding book launched Dav's career. He now has seven more books published.
Printed Full Color
ISBN 0-933849-22-2

by Karen Kerber, age 12
St. Louis, Missouri

A delightfully playful book! The text is loaded with clever alliterations and gentle humor. Karen's brightly colored illustrations are composed of wiggly and waggly strokes of genius.
Printed Full Color
ISBN 0-933849-29-X

Your Students Will Love These Wonderful Books!

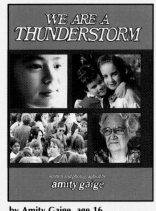

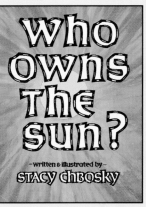
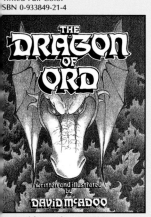

THE WINNERS OF THE 1992 NATIONAL
WRITTEN & ILLUSTRATED BY... AWARDS FOR STUDENTS

FIRST PLACE	**FIRST PLACE**	**FIRST PLACE**	**GOLD AWARD**	**GOLD AWARD**
6–9 Age Category	10–13 Age Category	14–19 Age Category	Publisher's Selection	Publisher's Selection
Benjamin Kendall	**Steven Shepard**	**Travis Williams**	**Dubravka Kolanovic'**	**Amy Jones**
age 7	age 13	age 16	age 18	age 17
State College, Pennsylvania	Great Falls, Virginia	Sardis, B.C., Canada	Savannah, Georgia	Shirley, Arkansas

ALIEN INVASIONS
When Ben puts on a new super-hero costume, he starts seeing Aliens who are from outer space. His attempts to stop the pesky invaders provide loads of laughs. The colorful illustrations add to the fun!

29 Pages, Full Color
ISBN 0-933849-42-7

FOGBOUND
A gripping thriller! When a boy rows his boat to an island to retrieve a stolen knife, he must face threatening fog, treacherous currents, and a sinister lobsterman. Outstanding illustrations!

29 Pages, Two-Color
ISBN 0-933849-43-5

CHANGES
A chilling mystery! When a teen-age boy discovers his classmates are missing, he becomes entrapped in a web of conflicting stories, false alibis, and frightening changes. Dramatic ink drawings!

29 Pages, Two-Color
ISBN 0-933849-44-3

A SPECIAL DAY
Ivan enjoys a wonderful day in the country with his grandparents, a dog, a cat, and a delightful bear that is *always* hungry. Cleverly written, brilliantly illustrated! Little kids will love this book!

29 Pages, Full Color
ISBN 0-933849-45-1

ABRACADABRA
A whirlwind adventure! An enchanted unicorn helps a young girl rescue her eccentric aunt from the evil Sultan of Zabar. A charming story, with lovely illustrations that add a magical glow!

29 Pages, Full Color
ISBN 0-933849-46-X

BOOKS FOR STUDENTS BY STUDENTS!®

Written &
Illustrated
by...

a revolutionary two-brain approach for teaching students how to write and illustrate amazing books

David Melton

Written & Illustrated by . . .
by David Melton

This highly acclaimed teacher's manual offers classroom-proven, step-by-step instructions in all aspects of teaching students how to write, illustrate, assemble, and bind original books. Loaded with information and positive approaches that really work. Contains lesson plans, more than 200 illustrations, and suggested adaptations for use at all grade levels — K through college.

The results are dazzling!
Children's Book Review Service, Inc.

WRITTEN & ILLUSTRATED BY... provides a current of enthusiasm, positive thinking and faith in the creative spirit of children. David Melton has the heart of a teacher.
THE READING TEACHER

...an exceptional book! Just browsing through it stimulates excitement for writing.
Joyce E. Juntune, Executive Director
The National Association for Creativity

A "how to" book that really works.
Judy O'Brien, Teacher

Softcover, 96 Pages
ISBN 0-933849-00-1

LANDMARK EDITIONS, INC.
P.O. BOX 4469 • KANSAS CITY, MISSOURI 64127 • (816) 241-4919

GRAFTON SCHOOL
P.O. Box 458
Knights Landing,
California 95645